AF573758

Seasons in the Meadow

First published in Great Britain in 1996 by
BROCKHAMPTON PRESS
20 Bloomsbury Street, London WC1B 3QA
a member of the Hodder Headline Group

This series of little gift books was made by Frances Banfield, Andrea P.A. Belloli, Polly Boyd, Kate Brown, Stefano Carantino, Laurel Clark, Penny Clarke, Clive Collins, Jack Cooper, Melanie Cumming, Nick Diggory, John Dunne, Deborah Gill, David Goodman, Paul Gregory, Douglas Hall, Lucinda Hawksley, Maureen Hill, Dennis Hovell, Dicky Howett, Nick Hutchison, Douglas Ingram, Helen Johnson, C.M. Lee, Simon London, Irene Lyford, John Maxwell, Patrick McCreeth, Morse Modaberi, Tara Neill, Sonya Newland, Anne Newman, Grant Oliver, Ian Powling, Terry Price, Michelle Rogers, Mike Seabrook, Nigel Soper, Karen Sullivan and Nick Wells.

ISBN 1 86019 477X
A copy of the CIP data is available from the British Library upon request.

Produced for Brockhampton Press by Flame Tree Publishing, a part of The Foundry Creative Media Company Limited, The Long House, Antrobus Road, Chiswick W4 5HY.

Printed and bound in Italy by L.E.G.O. Spa.

C E L E B R A T I O N

Seasons in the Meadow

Selected by Karen Sullivan

BROCKHAMPTON PRESS

Sherrin

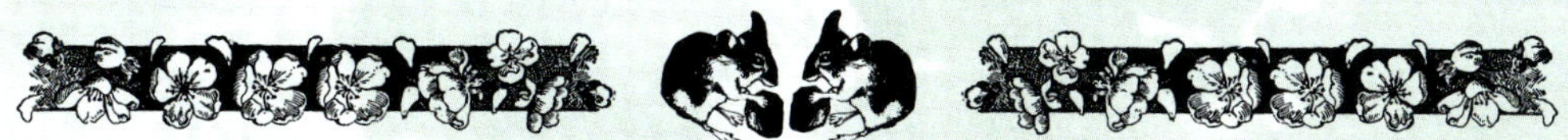

O to be in England
Now that April's here,
And whoever wakes in England
Sees, some morning, unaware,
That the lowest boughs and the brushwood sheaf
Round the elm-tree bole are in tiny leaf,
While the chaffinch sings on the orchard bough
In England – now!

Robert Browning, *'Home Thoughts from Abroad'*

The curfew tolls the knell of parting day,
The lowing herd winds slowly o'er the lea,
The ploughman homeward plods his weary way,
And leaves the world to darkness and to me.

Thomas Gray, *'Elegy Written in a Country Churchyard'*

Snowy, Flowy, Blowy,
Showery, Flowery, Bowery,
Hoppy, Croppy, Droppy,
Breezy, Sneezy, Freezy.

Sir George Gander, *The Twelve Months*

Or speak to the Earth, and it shall teach thee.

Job, XII:8

The green lakes are sleeping in the mountain shadow, and on the water's canvas bright sunshine paints the picture of the day.

Gwilym Cowlyd, *A Celtic Miscellany*

L. L.

A cherry year,
A merry year;
A pear year,
A dear year;
A plum year,
A dumb year.

Traditional

A pot of fresh basil
on the kitchen
windowsill keeps the
flies from entering.

Autumn wins you best by this its mute
Appeal to sympathy for its decay.

Robert Browning

This is the weather the cuckoo likes,
And so do I;
When showers betumble the chestnut spikes,
And nestlings fly...

Thomas Hardy, *'Weathers'*

Rough winds do shake the darling buds of May.

William Shakespeare

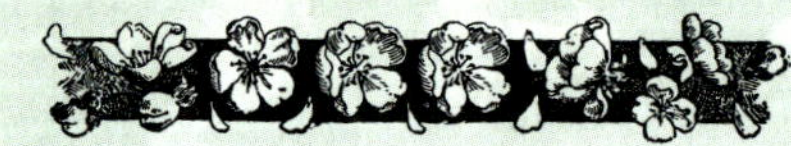

I was born under a kind star
In a green world withouten any war;
My eyes opened on quiet fields and hills,
Orchards and gardens, cowslips, daffodils,
Love for my rising-up and lying-down,
Amid the beautiful pastures green and brown –
The rose leaned through my window set ajar –
I was born under a kind star.

Katherine Tynana, *I Was Born Under a Kind Star*

Summer set lip to earth's bosom bare
And left the flushed print in a poppy there.

Francis Thompson

Between this half-wooded, half-naked hill, and the vague still horizon that its summit indistinctly commanded, was a mysterious sheet of fathomless shade – the sounds from which suggested that what it concealed bore some reduced resemblance to features here. The thin grasses, more or less coating the hill, were touched by the wind in breezes of differing powers, and almost of differing natures – one rubbing the blades heavily, another raking them piercingly, another brushing them like soft broom. The instinctive act of humankind was to stand and listen, and learn how the trees on the right and the trees on the left wailed or chaunted to each other in the regular antiphonies of a cathedral choir; how hedges and other shapes to leeward then caught the note, lowering it to the tenderest sob; and how the hurrying gust then plunged into the south, to be heard no more.

Thomas Hardy, *Far From the Madding Crowd*

I was at Kelmscott the other day, and betwixt fishing, I cut a handful of poplar twigs and boiled them, and dyed a lock of wool a very good yellow.

William Morris

Land is the only thing in the world that amounts to anything, for 'tis the only thing in this world that lasts... 'Tis the only thing worth working for, worth fighting for – worth dying for.

Margaret Mitchell, *Gone with the Wind*

Fallen leaves lying on the grass in the November sun bring more happiness than the daffodils.

Cyril Connolly

O, Wind,
If Winter comes, can Spring be far behind?

Percy Bysshe Shelley, *'Ode to the West Wind'*

A little dried lavender under the pillow brings a deep and dreamless sleep.

Traditional country remedy

O fret not after knowledge – I have none,
And yet my song comes native with the warmth.
O fret not after knowledge – I have none,
And yet the Evening listens.

John Keats, *'What the Thrush Said'*

Mrs Cherry's receipt for salade:

Two slices of onion very thin
One apple
Six chilies
One rather large raw tomato sliced
Half a beetroot well boiled and cold before being sliced
Two tablespoonfuls of vinegar
Two teaspoonfuls of salt.

'Tis the last rose of summer,
Left blooming alone;
All her lovely companions are faded and gone.

Thomas Moore

Cuckoo, cuckoo, what do you do?
In April I open my bill;
In May I sing all day;
In June I change my tune;
In July away I fly;
In August away I must.

Traditional

By shallow rivers, to whose falls,
Melodious birds sing madrigals.

Christopher Marlowe

Everywhere the branches of the willow bushes were tipped with downy white balls and the Alder-catkins were shewing very red.

An Edwardian lady's diary

Happier of happy though I be, like them
I cannot take possession of the sky,
Mount with a thoughtless impulse, and wheel there,
One of a mighty multitude whose way
And motion is a harmony and dance
Magnificent.

William Wordsworth

'Tis a dog's delight to bark and bite
And little birds to sing,
And if you sit on a red-hot brick
It's a sign of an early spring.

Anonymous

A swarm of bees in May
Is worth a load of hay;
A swarm of bees in June
Is worth a silver spoon;
A swarm of bees in July
Is not worth a fly.

Country saying

We need the tonic of wildness, to wade sometimes in marshes where the bittern and the meadow-hen lurk, and hear the booming of the snipe; to smell the whispering sedge where only some wilder and more solitary fowl builds her nest, and the mink crawls with its belly close to the ground.

Henry David Thoreau

The best remedy for those who are afraid, lonely or unhappy is to go outside, somewhere where they can be quiet, alone with the heavens, nature and God. Because only then does one feel that all is as it should be and that God wishes to see people happy, amidst the simple beauty of nature. As long as this exists, and it certainly always will, I know that then there will always be comfort for every sorrow, whatever the circumstances may be. And I firmly believe that nature brings solace in all troubles.

Anne Frank

However much you knock at nature's door, she will never answer you in comprehensible words.

Ivan Turgenev

To be interested in the changing seasons is, in this middling zone, a happier state of mind than to be hopelessly in love with spring.

George Santayana

The tree which moves some to tears of joy is in the eyes of others only a green thing that stands in the way. Some see nature all ridicule and deformity… and some scarce see nature at all. But to the eyes of the man of imagination, nature is imagination itself.

William Blake

A simple infusion of chamomile and yarrow flowers can be used to rinse fair hair to highlight the blonde colour.

The melancholy days are come, the saddest of the year,
Of wailing winds and naked woods, and meadows brown and sere.

William Cullen Bryant, *The Death of Flowers*

Live in each season as it passes; breathe the air, drink the drink, taste the fruit, and resign yourself to the influences of each. Let them be your only diet, drink and botanical medicines.

Henry David Thoreau

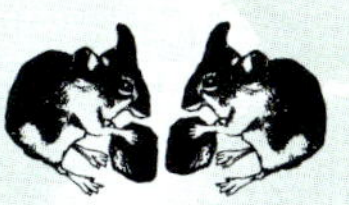

I was born upon thy bank, river,
My blood flows in thy stream,
And thou meanderest forever
At the bottom of my dream.

Henry David Thoreau

One day in the country
Is worth a month in town.

Christina Rossetti

To see the Summer Sky
Is Poetry, though never in a
    Book it lie –
True Poems flee.

Emily Dickinson

Rub a little salt on the hands to remove the odour of garlic and onions.

If the day and the night are such that you greet them with joy, and life emits a fragrance like flowers and sweet-scented herbs, is more elastic, more starry, more immortal – that is your success. All nature is your congratulation, and you have cause momentarily to bless yourself.

Henry David Thoreau

Make a freshening rosemary face rinse by boiling a handful of rosemary leaves and flowers in 300 ml (half pint) of water for 5 minutes. Leave to cool. Strain and pour into a screwtop bottle.

My aspens dear, whose airy cages quelled,
Quelled or quenched in leaves the leaping sun,
All felled, felled, are all felled;
Of a fresh and following folded rank
Not spared, not one
That dandled a sandalled
Shadow that swam or sank
On meadow and river and wind-wandering weed-
winding bank.

Gerard Manley Hopkins

Give fools their gold, and knaves their power;
Let fortune's bubbles rise and fall;
Who sows a field, or trains a flower,
Or plants a tree, is more than all.

John Greenleaf Whittier

S. BEWS

O suns and skies and clouds of June,
And flowers of June together,
Ye cannot rival for one hour
October's bright blue weather.

Helen Hunt Jackson

These flowers, which were splendid and sprightly,
Waking in the dawn of the morning,
In the evening will be a pitiful frivolity,
Sleeping in the cold night's arms.

Pedro Calderón de la Barca

For nature is so excellent in its gifts that… it better benefit a man to know one herb in the meadow, but to know it thoroughly, than to see the whole meadow without knowing what grows on it.

Paracelsus

I know no subject more elevating, more amazing, more ready to the poetical enthusiasm, the philosophical reflection, and the moral sentiment than the works of nature. Where can we meet such variety, such beauty, such magnificence?

James Thomson

For like as herbs and trees bringen forth fruit and flourish in May, in likewise every lusty heart that is in any manner a lover, springeth and flourisheth in lusty deeds.

Sir Thomas Malory

The lake looked to me, I knew not why, dull and melancholy, and the weltering on the shores seemed a heavy sound. I walked as long as I could amongst the stones of the shore. The wood rich in flowers; a beautiful yellow, palish flower, that looked thick, round, and double, and smelt very sweet – I supposed it was a ranunculus. Crowfoot, the grassy-leaved rabbit-toothed white flower, strawberries, geranium, scentless violets, anemones two kinds, orchids, primroses. The heckberry very beautiful, the crab coming out as a low shrub. Met a blind man, driving a very large beautiful Bull, and a cow – he walked with two sticks. Came home by Clappersgate. The valley very green; many sweet views up to Rydale head...

Dorothy Wordsworth, Journal entry, 14 May 1800

Fresh Herb Dressing

1 heaped tsp sugar
a pinch each of mustard, pepper and salt
1 tsp of French wine vinegar
2-3 tsp best olive oil or cream
chopped chives, parsley, thyme, mint, marjoram, and sage
Mix some hours before serving.

Who has seen the wind?
Neither you nor I:
But when the trees bow down their heads,
The wind is passing by.

Christina Rossetti

My Sorrow, when she's here with me,
Thinks these dark days of autumn rain
Are beautiful as days can be;
She loves the bare, the withered tree;
She walks the sodden pasture lane.

Robert Frost

A tree of apples – great its bounty!
Like a hostel, vast!
A pretty bush, thick as a fist,
    of tiny hazelnuts
A green mass of branches.

Dillon, *Early Irish Literature*

O why do you walk through the fields in gloves,
Missing so much and so much?
O fat white woman whom nobody loves,
Why do you walk through the fields in gloves
When the grass is soft as the breast of doves
And shivering sweet to the touch?

Frances Cornford, *To a Fat Lady Seen from a Train*

And sloes dim-covered as with dewy veils
And rambling bramble berries plump and sweet
Arching their prickly trails
Half o'er the narrow lane.

John Clare

...Therefore am I still
A lover of the meadows and the woods,
And mountains...

William Wordsworth, *'Lines Composed a Few Miles above Tintern Abbey'*

No shade, no shine, no butterflies, no bees,
No fruits, no flowers, no leaves, no birds, –
November!

Thomas Hood, *No!*

There will come soft rains and the smell of the ground,
And swallows calling with their shimmering sound;

Sara Teasdale, *There Will Come Soft Rains*

The Lord is my shepherd
I have everything I need.
He lets me rest in fields of green
And leads me to quiet pools of
    fresh water.

Psalms, XXIII:1

Will you find me an acre of land –
Parsley, Sage, Rosemary and Thyme –
Between the sea foam and the
    sea sand?
You shall be a true love of mine.

Anonymous, *'Scarborough Fair'*

When icicles hang by the wall
And Dick the shepherd blows his nail
And Tom bears logs into the hall,
And milk comes frozen home in pail,
When blood is nipped and ways be foul,
Then nightly sings the staring owl,
Tu-who;
Tu-whit, tu-who: a merry note,
While greasy Joan doth keel the pot.

William Shakespeare, *Love's Labours Lost*

When daisies pied and violets blue,
And lady-smocks all silver white,
And cuckoo buds of yellow hue,
Do paint the meadows with delight.

William Shakespeare, *Love's Labours Lost*

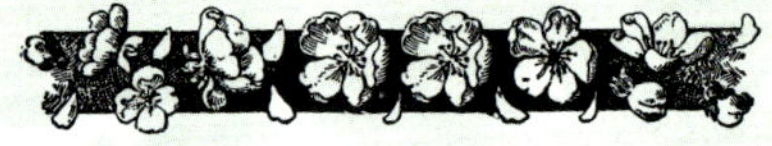

Mammalia Pl.11.

The essence of an herbal ritual is in the reverence and intent that you bring to it. Choose your herbs with care, and always leave a gift for the earth when you take one of her plant children: a pinch of vervain, tobacco, or corn meal, or a gift of new honey or cider.

A Druid's Herbal

Four Seasons fill the measure of the year;
There are four seasons in the mind of man…

John Keats, *'The Human Seasons'*

How could such sweet and wholesome hours
Be reckoned but with herbs and flowers?

Andrew Marvel, *'The Garden'*

Get up, sweet slug-a-bed, and see
The dew bespangling herb and tree.

Robert Herrick, *'Corinna's Gone a-Maying'*

I sing of brooks, of blossoms, birds and bowers,
Of April, May, of June and July-flowers.

Robert Herrick, *'The Argument of His Book'*

Each smooth nut puts forth its shell at the end of its branch on the margin of the corn land: the yellow grain dons its husk underneath a fresh bending brake.

Dillon, *Early Irish Literature*

Look after your sheep and cattle as carefully as you can, because wealth is not permanent.

Proverb

Golden lie the meadows; golden run the streams... the sun is coming down to earth and walks the fields and the waters.

George Meredith, *The Ordeal of Richard Feverel*

I know a bank where the wild thyme blows,
Where oxlips and the nodding violet grows
Quite over-canopied with luscious woodbine,
With sweet musk-roses, and with eglantine:
There sleeps Titania some time of the night,
Lull'd by these flowers with dances and delight;
And there the snake throws her enamell'd skin,
Weed wide enough to wrap a fairy in.

William Shakespeare, *A Midsummer-Night's Dream*

Next, let the planter with discretion meet
The force and genius of each soil explore,
To what adapted, what it shuns averse.

John Philips, *Cyder*

Ne needs there Gardiner to set, or sow,
To plant or prune: for of their owne accord
All things, as they created were, doe grow.

Edmund Spenser, *'The Fairie Queene'*

When as the rye reach to the chin,
And chopcherry, chopcherry ripe within,
Strawberries swimming in the cream,
And schoolboys playing in the stream.

George Peele, *A Summer Song*

Meadows trim with daisies pied,
Shallow brooks and rivers wide.

John Milton, *'L'Allegro'*

When dusty summer bakes the crumbling clods
How pleasant is't beneath the twist'd arch
Of a retreating bower in mid-day's reign,
To ply the sweet carouse, remote from noise,
Secur'd of feverish heats!

John Philips, *Cyder*

Spring, the sweet spring, is the year's pleasant king;
Then blooms each thing, then maids dance in a ring,
Cold doth not sting, and the pretty birds do sing:
Cuckoo, jug-jug, pu-we, to-witta-woo!

Thomas Nashe, *'Spring'*

Every flower is a soul blossoming in Nature.

Gérard de Nerval

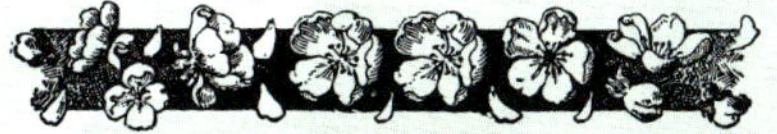

January gray is here,
Like a sexton by her grave;
February bears the bier,
March with grief doth howl and rave,
And April weeps – but, O ye hours!
Follow with May's fairest flowers.

Percy Bysshe Shelley

Summer is y-comen in,
Loude sing, cuckoo!
Groweth seed, and bloweth meed
And spring'th the woode new.

Anonymous, *'Summer is y-Comen In'*

When the moonlight
Starts to seep
Through the trees,
Autumn has come
With trouble, with care.

Anonymous, *When the Moonlight*

Harvest moon,
And mist creeping
Over the water.

Haiku by Hattori Rasetsu

I feel I can not propose in London… we must go for a day in the country and when surrounded by the gay twittering of the birds and the smell of the cows I will lay my suit at her feet.

Daisy Ashford, *The Young Visitors*

An industrial worker would sooner have a £5 note but a countryman must have praise.

Ronald Blythe, *Akenfield*

Many of the phenomena of Winter are suggestive of an inexpressible tenderness and fragile delicacy. We are accustomed to hear this king described as a rude and boisterous tyrant; but with the gentleness of a lover he adorns the tresses of Summer.

Henry David Thoreau

A fir-tree once boasted to a bramble: 'You're good for nothing at all; but without me no one could build a barn or a house.' 'My dear man,' answered the bramble, 'just you wait till the woodmen come along, and then see whether you'd rather be a bramble or a fir.'

Aesop, *'The Fir-Tree and the Bramble'*

The great events of life often leave one unmoved; they pass out of consciousness, and, when one thinks of them, become unreal. Even the scarlet flowers of passion seem to grow in the same meadow as the poppies of oblivion.

Oscar Wilde

And meadow rivulets overflow,
And drops on gate-bars hang in a row,
And rooks in families homeward go,
And so do I.

Thomas Hardy, *Late Lyrics*

Loveliest of trees, the cherry now,
Is hung with bloom along the bough,
And stands about the woodland ride,
Wearing white for Eastertide.

A. E. Housman, *'A Shropshire Lad'*

Before the gods that made the gods
Had seen their sunrise pass,
The White Horse of the White Horse Vale,
Was cut out of the grass.

G. K. Chesterton, *Ballad of the White Horse*

The naked earth is warm with Spring,
And with green grass and bursting trees
Leans to the sun's kiss glorying,
And quivers in the sunny breeze.

Julian Grenfell, *Into Battle*

What is one to say about June – the time of perfect young summer, the fulfilment of the promise of the earlier months, and with as yet no sign to remind one that its young fresh beauty will ever fade? For my own part I wander up into the wood and say 'June is here – June is here; thank God for lovely June!' The soft cooing of the wood-dove, the glad song of many birds, the flitting of butterflies, the hum of all the little winged people among the branches, the sweet earth-scents – all seem to say the same, with an endless reiteration, never wearying because so gladsome. It is the offering of the Hymn of Praise!

Gertrude Jekyll, *June*

It is not spring until you can plant your foot upon twelve daisies.

Proverb

What is a butterfly? At best
He's but a caterpillar dressed.

Benjamin Franklin, *Poor Richard's Almanac*

I've watched you now a full half-hour,
Self-poised upon that yellow flower;
And, little Butterfly! indeed
I know not if you sleep or feed.
How motionless! and then
What joy awaits you, when the breeze
Hath found you out among the trees,
And calls you forth again!

William Wordsworth, *'To a Butterfly'*

...Lay her in the earth:
And from her fair and unpolluted flesh
May violets spring.

William Shakespeare, *Hamlet*

The kiss of the sun for pardon,
The song of the birds for mirth,
One is nearer God's Heart in a garden
Than anywhere else on earth.

Dorothy Frances Gurney

Kissing with golden face the meadows green,
Gilding pale streams with heavenly alchemy.

William Shakespeare, *'Sonnet'*

Little maid, pretty maid, whither goest thou?
Down in the meadow to milk my cow.
Shall I go with thee? No, not now;
When I send for thee, then come thou.

English nursery rhyme

I have sown upon the fields
Eyebright and Pimpernel
And Pansy and Poppy-seed
Ripen'd and scatter'd well,

And silver Lady-smock
The meads with light to fill
Cowslip and Buttercup,
Daisy and Daffodil;

King-cup and Fleur-de-lys
Upon the marsh to meet
With Comfrey, Watermint,
Loose-strife and Meadowsweet;

And all along the stream
My care hath not forgot
Crowsfoot's white galaxy
And love's Forget-me-not:

And where high grasses wave
Shall great Moon-daisies blink,
With Rattle and Sorrel sharp
And Robin's ragged pink.

Thick on the woodland floor
Gay company shall be,
Primrose and Hyacinth
And frail Anemone.

Perennial Strawberry-bloom
Woodsorrel's pencilled veil
Dishevel'd Willow-weed
And Orchis purple pale.

Robert Bridges, *The Idle Flowers*

Ask of her, the mighty mother:
Her reply puts this other
Question: What is Spring? –
Growth in everything.

Gerard Manley Hopkins

When swift cloud shadows race over the hills –
Where tinkling water leaps down the steep ghylls
On wide brown sands at the edge of the sea –
Little odd people come whisper to me!

Under the bracken and wood moss they peep,
And play in the moonlight when other folks sleep,
They hide in the sweet-smelling hay in the barn,
And under the wainscots and tubs at the farm.

Land of kind dreams where the mountains are blue,
Where brownies are friendly and wishing comes true!
Through your green meadows they dance hand in hand –
Little odd people of Buttercup Land.

Beatrix Potter, *Buttercup Land*

Notes on Illustrations

Page 1 *Rabbits* by John Sherrin (Victoria and Albert Museum, London) Courtesy of The Bridgeman Art Library; **Page 3** *Little Girl on a Knoll* Courtesy of The Laurel Clark Collection; **Pages 4-5** *Foxes Waiting for the Prey* by Carl Friedrich Deiker (Gavin Graham Gallery, London) Courtesy of The Bridgeman Art Library; **Page 7** *An Autumn Afternoon* by Charles James Adams (Fine-Lines (Fine Art), Warwickshire) Courtesy of The Bridgeman Art Library; **Page 8** *Cottage in a Cornfield* by John Constable (Victoria and Albert Museum, London) Courtesy of The Bridgeman Art Library; **Page 13** *Castle Coch, South Wales:* Detail of the Mural in the Drawing Room showing 'The Quack Doctor' by William Burgess (John Bethnell) Courtesy of The Bridgeman Art Library; **Page 14** *Towards Evening in the Forest* by Henry William Banks Davis (Christopher Wood Gallery, London) Courtesy of The Bridgeman Art Library; **Pages 16-17** *Grey Fox* by John James Audubon (Natural History Museum, London) Courtesy of The Bridgeman Art Library; **Page 19** *Field Mice at the Foot of the Tree* by George Thomas Rope (Waterhouse and Dodd, London) Courtesy of The Bridgeman Art Library; **Pages 20-1** *The Gate* by Brian Sanders (Artist's Collection) Courtesy of The Bridgeman Art Library; **Page 25** *Picnic* Courtesy of The Laurel Clark Collection; Pages 26-7 *Family of Hedgehogs* by Seigmar Jugelt (Josef Mensing Gallery, Hamm-Rhynern) Courtesy of The Bridgeman Art Library; **Page 28** *A View Near Sefton, Lancashire* by John Edward Newton (Roy Miles Gallery, 29 Bruton Street, London) Courtesy of The Bridgeman Art Library; **Page 31** *The Joys of Nature* by Susie Bews (Private Collection) Courtesy of The Bridgeman Art Library; **Page 32** *Twilight* by William J. Webb (Private Collection) Courtesy of The Bridgeman Art Library; **Page 36** *Three Little Girls* Courtesy of The Laurel Clark Collection; **Pages 38-9** *The Fox* by English School (Ackermann and Johnson Ltd., London) Courtesy of The Bridgeman Art Library; **Page 41** *Fox and Cubs* by Sue Warner (Private Collection) Courtesy of The Bridgeman Art Library; **Page 42** *Landscape* by Pierre Auguste Renoir (Christie's, London) Courtesy of The Bridgeman Art Library; **Pages 44-5** *The Gleaners* by Jean-Francois Millet (Louvre, Paris). Courtesy of The Bridgeman Art Library; **Page 47** *Two Field Mice from 'Zoology from the Voyage of the Beagle'* by Charles Darwin (Biblioteque Nationale, Paris) Courtesy of The Bridgeman Art Library; **Page 49** *Rabbits by a Burrow* by Charles Whymper (Chris Beetles Ltd., London) Courtesy of The Bridgeman Art Library; **Page 51** *Badger* by Francis Barlow (Roy Miles Gallery, 29 Bruton Street, London) Courtesy of The Bridgeman Art Library; **Page 52** *Path in the Long Grass* by Pierre Auguste Renoir (Louvre, Paris) Courtesy of The Bridgeman Art Library; **Page 55** *Otter* by Sue Warner (Private Collection) Courtesy of The Bridgeman Art Library; **Page 59** *Picking Flowers* Courtesy of The Laurel Clark Collection; **Pages 60-1** *An Artful Dodger* by T. B. Whaite (Bonhams, London) Courtesy of The Bridgeman Art Library; **Page 63** *Rabbit* by Sue

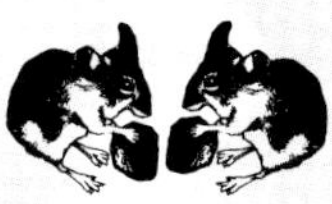

Warner (Private Collection) Courtesy of The Bridgeman Art Library; **Pages 64-5** *Shrews* by Edward Lear (Private Collection) Courtesy of The Bridgeman Art Library; **Page 67** *The Rabbit* by Conrad Franz (Josef Mensing Gallery, Hamm-Rhynern) Courtesy of The Bridgeman Art Library; **Page 68** *Girl and Goat* Courtesy of The Laurel Clark Collection; **Page 71** *The Entrance to Fen Lane* by John Constable (Phillips, The International Fine Art Auctioneers). Courtesy of The Bridgeman Art Library; **Page 72** *Eluding the Fox* by Bruno Liljefors (Julian Simon Fine Art Ltd.) Courtesy of The Bridgeman Art Library; **Pages 74-5** *Dormice* by Edward Lear (Private Collection) Courtesy of The Bridgeman Art Library. **Page 77** *Someone Run and Find Bo-Peep* Courtesy of The Laurel Clark Collection; **Pages 80-1** *The Sheep Drover* by O. T. Clark (The Standberg Cove Gallery, London) Courtesy of The Bridgeman Art Library; **Page 82** *Daisy Chains* Courtesy of The Laurel Clark Collection.

Acknowledgements: The Publishers wish to thank everyone who gave permission to reproduce the quotes in this book. Every effort has been made to contact the copyright holders, but in the event that an oversight has occurred, the publishers would be delighted to rectify any omissions in future editions of this book. *Gone with the Wind* © Margaret Mitchell, 1936; *A Druid's Herbal* © Ellen Evert Hopman, 1995, published by Destiny Books, Rochester, Vermont; *Dorothy Wordsworth's Journals* reprinted courtesy of William Collins Sons & Co Ltd, © Robert Ditchfield Ltd, 1987; Robert Frost reprinted from *The Poetry of Robert Frost,* by permission of Jonathan Cape and the Estate of Robert Frost, and Peter A. Gilbert, North Hampshire, USA; Beatrix Potter reprinted courtesy of Frederick Warne Limited, Penguin Books © Frederick Warne, copyright renewed; G. K. Chesterton reprinted courtesy of Methuen and Dodd Mead, copyright renewed; Thomas Hardy reprinted courtesy of Viking Penguin; Sarah Teasdale from *Collected Poems 1928-1953,* published by Macmillan © 1915 renewed 1943 by Mamie T. Wheless. Reprinted with permission of Macmillan Publishing Co. Ltd; *Good News Study Bible,* published by Thomas Nelson, 1986, extracts reprinted with their kind permission; *Penguin Book of Japanese Verse,* translated by Geoffrey Bownas and Anthony Thwaite, published by Penguin 1964, and reprinted with their permission.